OCD - Tools to Help You Fight Back!

by the same author

Breaking Free from OCD
A CBT Guide for Young People and Their Families
Jo Derisley, Isobel Heyman, Sarah Robinson and Cynthia Turner
ISBN 978 1 84310 574 9
eISBN 978 1 84642 799 2

of related interest

Understanding OCD
A Guide for Parents and Professionals
Edited by Adam B. Lewin and Eric A. Storch
ISBN 978 1 84905 783 7
eISBN 978 1 78450 026 9

Can I tell you about OCD?
A guide for friends, family and professionals
Amita Jassi
Illustrated by Sarah Hull
ISBN 978 1 84905 381 5
eISBN 978 0 85700 736 0
Part of the *Can I tell you about...?* series

OCD - Tools to Help You

FIGHT BACK!

A CBT Workbook for Young People

CYNTHIA TURNER, GEORGINA KREBS AND CHLOË VOLZ

Illustrated by Lisa Jo Robinson

Jessica Kingsley *Publishers*
London and Philadelphia

First published in 2019
by Jessica Kingsley Publishers
73 Collier Street
London N1 9BE, UK
and
400 Market Street, Suite 400
Philadelphia, PA 19106, USA

www.jkp.com

Library of Congress Cataloging in Publication Data
A CIP catalog record for this book is available from the Library of Congress

British Library Cataloguing in Publication Data
A CIP catalogue record for this book is available from the British Library

ISBN 978 1 84905 402 7
eISBN 978 0 85700 770 4

Printed and bound in Great Britain

Acknowledgements

There are many people who have contributed to the development of this programme. These include other professionals working in the field of childhood OCD, and many of the staff and trainees who have worked at the OCD, BDD and Related Disorders Clinic for Young People at the Maudsley Hospital. Special thanks to Isobel Heyman, who was central in helping to develop and refine many of the concepts and materials that are used here during her time as consultant psychiatrist of the OCD team at the Maudsley. We are very grateful to the therapists who were involved with our treatment trials using this workbook and manual, particularly Caroline Stokes, Holly Diamond, Jacinda Cadman and Amita Jassi. The more recent process of revising and updating these materials has truly been a team effort and in particular we would like to thank Benedetta Monzani for her many hours of work drafting new sheets and checking and cross-checking both publications. In addition, thanks go to Gazal Jones, Victoria Hallett and Angela Lewis for all their helpful hard work and contributions. Most importantly, we would like to thank the many children and families we have worked with who have contributed so much to our knowledge and understanding of OCD and its treatment.

Lastly, we would like to thank the funding bodies that have enabled us to test and refine this treatment manual and workbook. We are grateful to the Maudsley Charity, the National Institute for Health Research (NIHR) Patients Benefit (RfPB) Programme (grant reference number PB-PG-0107-12333) and the NIHR Maudsley Biomedical Research Centre grant for funding research trials that evaluated the effectiveness of this intervention. We are also grateful to the Medical Research Council who funded Georgina Krebs's Clinical Research Training Fellowship (reference number MR/N001400/1).

Table of contents

Cognitive Behaviour Therapy (CBT) for OCD

You will be offered up to 14 sessions in 8–17 weeks (you may not need that many).

This treatment involves working with a therapist to fight your OCD through a step-by-step process. We aim to be flexible and collaborative in the way we work with you, while at the same time sticking to an overall structure that we know works well.

Sessions 1–2	**Education.** This is where you and your family will learn more about OCD and how it works, and in particular the role that anxiety plays in keeping it going.
Sessions 3–6	**Exposure and response prevention (ERP).** After making a list of all the things that OCD makes you do (a hierarchy), you will then begin to try and stop, delay or mess up some of your rituals, with lots of help and support from your therapist and any family members who may be involved in helping. You may do some of these tasks at the clinic but you will also need to practise these every day at home.
Session 7	**Review** and measure OCD again.
Sessions 8–13	Continue fighting your OCD with **regular ERP tasks** both at the clinic and at home.
Session 14	**Relapse prevention.** We will work with you to make sure that you know what to do if OCD tries to come back.
Follow-up appointments	When you have finished your regular treatment, you will be offered four follow-up appointments over 12 months. These will be at one month, three months, six months and 12 months after treatment has ended.
Measurements	An important part of CBT is to measure the change that is taking place in order to see how you are progressing and how your recovery is impacting on your life and your family. You will have already completed initial measures and these will be repeated at the end of your treatment, and again at three months, six months and 12 months after treatment.

A word about commitment to treatment...

We know that fighting OCD is tough and sometimes when you start fighting you can feel a bit worse before you feel better, but we are here to support you. Although you may not always feel like it, if you can attend every session and carry out daily tasks at home then you will make much quicker and better progress. Deciding to fight your OCD is a big commitment but it is worth it!

WHAT IS OCD?

- OCD stands for obsessive compulsive disorder.

- Obsessions are thoughts, or worries, or pictures in our mind.

- Obsessions are not very nice, and they are not wanted.

- Compulsions are actions or things that we do. Sometimes we do them to try and make the obsessions go away. Sometimes OCD just makes us feel like we have to do certain things.

- OCD is quite common and it affects one or two in every 100 young people.

Some common obsessions are:

- fears about dirt or contamination
- worrying about harm coming to yourself or others
- unwanted sexual thoughts
- thoughts about doing something forbidden or embarrassing
- worrying if things are symmetrical or even
- needing to tell, ask or confess
- fear of losing important things
- doubts and urges.

Some common compulsions are:

checking

tricks to cancel thoughts

'evening up'

seeking reassurance

hoarding

Putting things 'just right'

repeating

washing

counting

arranging

WHAT CAUSES OCD?

- No one knows definitely what causes OCD.

- No one is to blame for OCD. It is not your fault that you have got OCD, and it is not your parents' fault.

- What we do know about OCD is that there are some things which might make people more sensitive to OCD than others.

- Some of the things which make people more sensitive to getting OCD are:

  - worrying too much if you get a bad or unpleasant thought

  - having a family 'risk' of OCD

  - the balance of a brain chemical called serotonin

  - stresses in your life.

- Whatever it is that causes OCD, we know that OCD works by tricking us into doing things that it wants us to do! OCD tricks us into thinking and feeling in certain ways.

For example, OCD tricks us into worrying more than other people, or worrying about things that other people don't worry about (these worries are called **obsessions**).

OCD also tricks us into doing certain things by making us feel scared or uncomfortable. The things that OCD tricks us into doing are called **compulsions**. Usually compulsions are normal behaviours that everyone does, but OCD 'tricks' us into doing them more often or in unusual ways. (Sometimes compulsions are also called **rituals**.)

Tools for fighting OCD

TOOL 1: EXTERNALISING OCD

Recognise that OCD is a problem (it is separate from you)

OCD is a lot like a bully. Sometimes children or young people like to give OCD a name or draw what OCD looks like to them. Others may prefer to write a little bit about what OCD is like for them. Some people like to note down some descriptive words that come to mind when thinking about OCD.

 Use this space to give OCD a name, to draw OCD, to write about what it is like or just to note down some descriptive words that come to mind.

Tools for fighting OCD

TOOL 2: UNDERSTANDING ANXIETY

Anxiety is a normal feeling that everyone has from time to time. When we feel anxious, we usually get changes in our body to help us understand how we are feeling.

 What happens to your body when you feel anxious or worried about something? Let's make a list of how you feel anxiety affects you in your body:

e.g. Headache
Feel sick

- Anxiety is a helpful emotion. It helps us to face up to real dangers.

- This response is known as the fight or flight response.

- Can you think of examples of where this is true for animals? For example, a zebra seeing a hungry lion racing in.

- Can you think of examples of where this is true for humans? This response is often illustrated in movies (*The Titanic*, war movies, even Harry Potter stories and movies).

- Can you think of an example where our body responds using the fight or flight response unnecessarily? For example, the noise of a cat in the night or stepping on the garden hose in the dark.

- Can you think of a time when you were feeling frightened of something and then these feelings went away when you realised there was really nothing to be afraid of?

- Different kinds of situations and things cause us to feel anxious or worried.

- But some things cause us to feel more anxious than other things!

- Let's use this rating scale to help us think about our feelings of anxiety.

- A 0 on the scale would be not at all anxious or worried. We might feel totally relaxed, like when we are sitting on a comfortable couch watching our favourite TV show!

- A 10 on the scale would be the most anxious you could possibly imagine feeling! It is likely to be in a life-threatening situation!

We can use this rating scale to help us rate our anxiety in different situations!

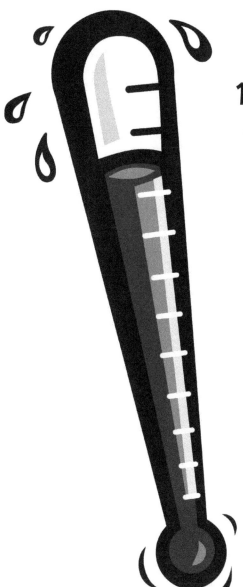

10 really, really anxious and awful

9

8 very anxious

7

6 medium anxious

5

4 somewhat anxious

3

2 a bit anxious

1

0 not anxious at all

Making your anxiety rating scale

- Think of some (non-OCD) things in your life that make you feel anxious.

- For example, you might be anxious about presenting a talk in front of your class, anxious about walking home alone when it is dark, or anxious about performing in the school play.

- Let's begin to rate these fears. To do this, think about how anxious you would feel if you did do the thing you feel afraid of.

- Write those things on your scale next to the right number.

- Now you have a ruler to measure your OCD by.

What happens to anxiety over time: Anxiety habituation

■ Let's have a look at how anxiety works. When we think about doing something that we feel anxious or worried about (for example, performing in front of an audience such as acting in a play or giving a speech), the feelings of anxiety that we get in our body are HUGE! They rise up really quickly, we feel scared, and we almost think that we can't go ahead with it!

■ But even though it's a really hard thing to do, we make ourselves do it, and when we do, we realise that it is not so scary after all! Then our feelings of anxiety just pass.

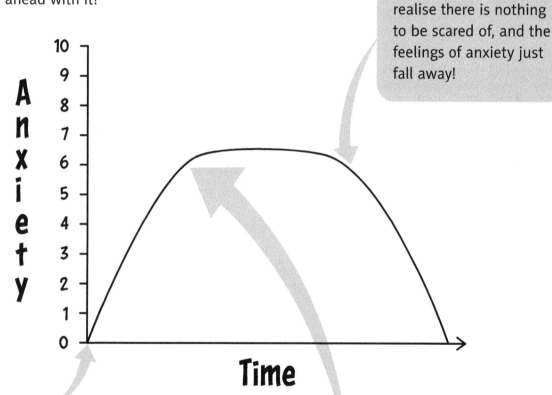

If we stick it out, we realise there is nothing to be scared of, and the feelings of anxiety just fall away!

At the start, we feel REALLY scared, and our feelings of anxiety go up very quickly!

Then we get to a point when our feelings 'peak' and they just don't go up any more. They kind of level off. This is where we have to make sure that we stick it out and don't change our mind!

■ Let's imagine that we keep performing in the same play over and again for several nights in a row.

■ The first night, our feelings of anxiety are REALLY high! But we stick it out, and like we just saw, the feelings of anxiety pass away!

■ When we go on stage the second time, we still feel quite scared, but not as scared as the opening night. And when we stick it out, the feelings pass away even sooner than before.

■ If we perform in the same play over and over again, each time we do it, our feelings of anxiety are not so bad, and they pass away even more quickly. If we do it enough times, we begin not to feel anxious at all!

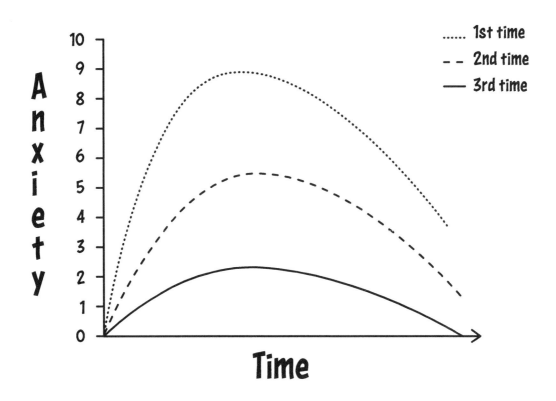

First time	The first time we do it, we feel really anxious!
Second time	The second time, our feelings are not quite so bad.
Third time	The third time, they are not quite so bad again! If we keep going, the feelings keep getting smaller and smaller, and then we don't feel anxious at all!

What happens to anxiety in OCD?

- When OCD makes us feel anxious, we usually do a compulsion or ritual to bring the anxiety down quickly.

- The problem is, over time, OCD starts to make us feel more anxious and demands more compulsions to bring our anxiety down.

- Over time it can get hard to satisfy OCD. Has this happened to you?

- Remember that the earlier graph reminds us that anxiety comes down over time, even without doing a ritual, and the more we practise not doing the ritual, the easier it gets.

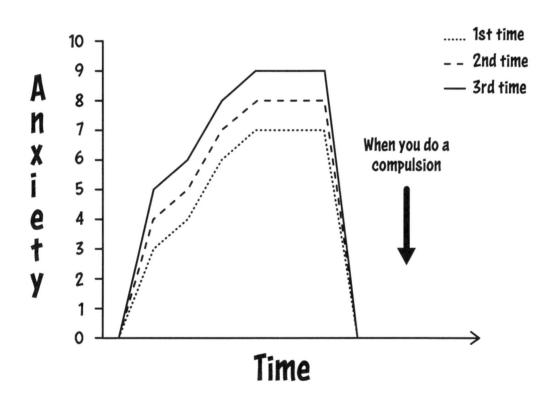

YOU CAN RESIST OCD

- There are times when it feels like OCD will always boss us around and make us do things we don't want to do.

- But there are also times when we can be the boss of OCD.

- Can you think of a time over the past few weeks when you were able to resist doing something that OCD wanted you to do?

- Maybe you simply had no time, or you were too tired, or someone who usually helps you do a ritual wasn't there.

- Maybe you didn't completely resist the OCD, but you were able to partially resist by doing something a little differently.

 I was able to resist OCD when:

HOMEWORK: SESSION 1

■ Read over Session 1.

■ Finish drawing, naming OCD (page 14) (optional).

■ Be an 'anxiety detective': notice anxiety symptoms in your body this week and fill in the boxes on page 15.

■ Finish your anxiety rating scale.

■ Think about three times when you have been able to resist OCD.

■ Other homework:

_____

_____

_____

_____

_____

_____

_____

■ Write three things you learned/will remember from Session 1:

_____

_____

_____

■ Write any questions here that you want to ask next time. Is there anything you want to know or learn more about?

_____

_____

_____

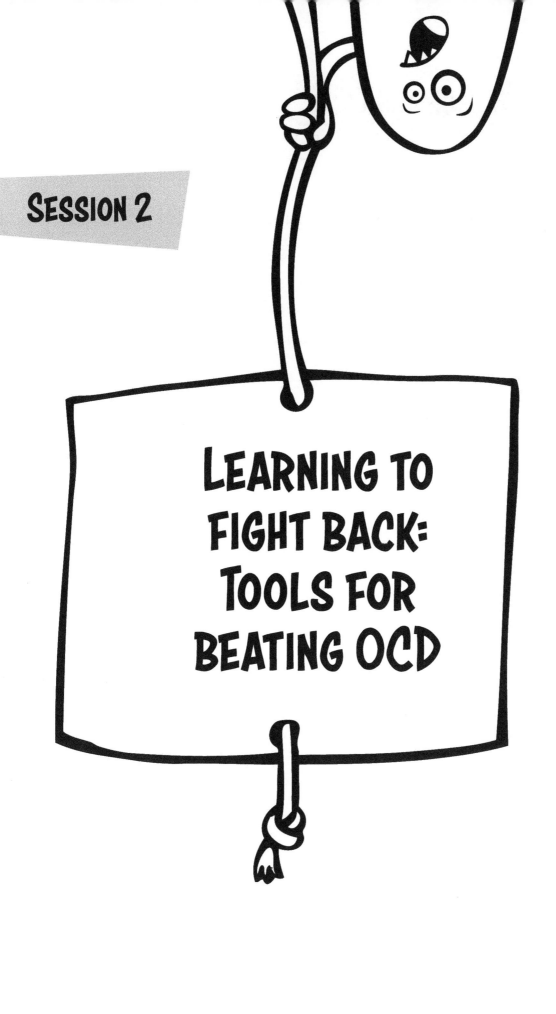

LEARNING TO FIGHT BACK: TOOLS FOR BEATING OCD

TOOLS FOR FIGHTING OCD

Recap: What have you learned so far?

In Session 1 you learned your first two tools for fighting OCD:

- **Tool 1:** Externalising OCD

- **Tool 2:** Understanding anxiety by recognising how anxiety feels in your body, rating anxiety on a 0–10 scale and knowing that anxiety comes down over time.

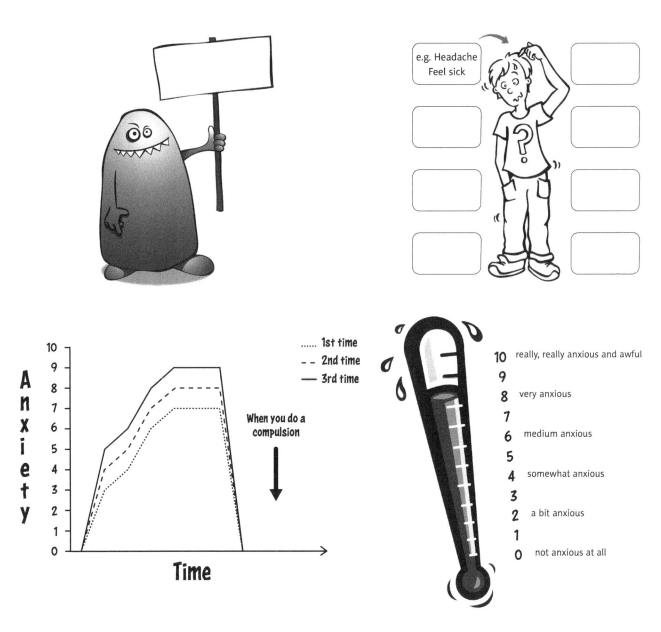

In Session 2 you will learn:

- **Tool 3:** Making an OCD hierarchy

- **Tool 4:** The OCD cycle.

Tools for fighting OCD

TOOL 3: MAKING AN OCD HIERARCHY

- First, write down the compulsions or habits that OCD makes you do. Don't forget the things that you 'do' in your head – we call these mental rituals.

- Then, think about the things that you AVOID doing because of OCD. What is OCD stopping you from doing that you should be able to do (e.g. going into certain rooms, touching certain things, speaking about particular things)? Your OCD list should include these avoidance behaviours.

- Write all these in the compulsion column.

- Then, think about whether OCD makes you do any things just because it 'feels right'.

- Last, list things that other people (friends, family, teachers) are doing for your OCD. If there are lots of things that other people are doing for your OCD, you may find it helpful to look at Tool 8 (Reassurance seeking and accommodation of OCD) (page 112).

- Once you have listed all your compulsions, then think about **how anxious you would feel if you were asked to resist doing these compulsions** (i.e. if you couldn't do what your OCD wanted you to do). Use the anxiety rating scale to help with this.

COMPULSION What is the habit or ritual? Is there anything you avoid doing/ touching? Don't forget the things you 'do' in your head.	ANXIETY RATING How anxious would you feel if you could not do the compulsion?

Tool 3: Making an OCD Hierarchy continued

■ Once you have given each of your compulsions an anxiety rating, you might like to put them into rank order. This means starting with the item that you would find the easiest to resist, and continuing until you have entered the item that you would find the hardest to resist at the top.

■ Now you have an OCD hierarchy!

Top of the hierarchy (hardest things)

Anxiety rating (0–10)

Bottom of the hierarchy (easiest things)

A NOTE ABOUT HORRIBLE THOUGHTS IN OCD

We usually start the fight against OCD by tackling the things that we are doing for OCD, or the things we are avoiding because of OCD (the compulsions), but sometimes young people say that the worst part of their OCD is the horrible thoughts (obsessions) that they are having.

If you would like to know more about horrible thoughts in OCD and how to tackle them, then you and your therapist can look at Tools 9 and 10 on pages 114–119 in this workbook.

Tools for fighting OCD

TOOL 4: THE OCD CYCLE

How does OCD work?

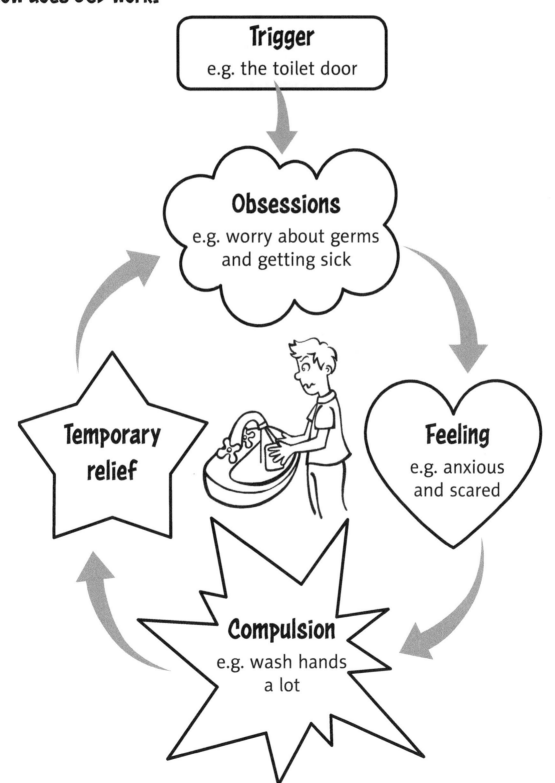

Trigger
e.g. the toilet door

Obsessions
e.g. worry about germs and getting sick

Temporary relief

Feeling
e.g. anxious and scared

Compulsion
e.g. wash hands a lot

Use this page to think of an example of how your OCD works.

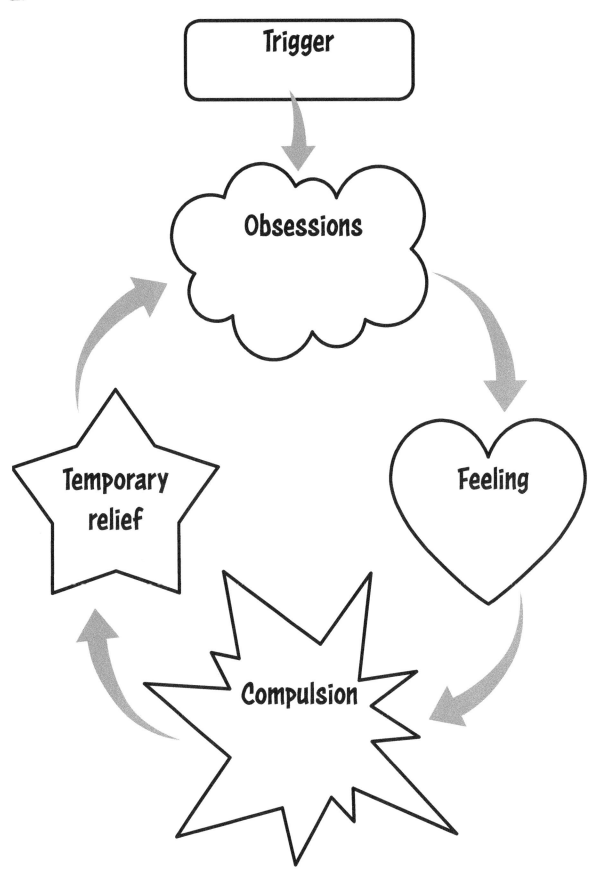

Trigger

Obsessions

Temporary relief

Feeling

Compulsion

■ So, before you turn the page, think about how and where you might break this cycle and how to begin fighting back against OCD.

How to break the OCD cycle

Many people want to take away the trigger, or to stop the thoughts, but the only part of the cycle that you can control is behaviours (the compulsions).

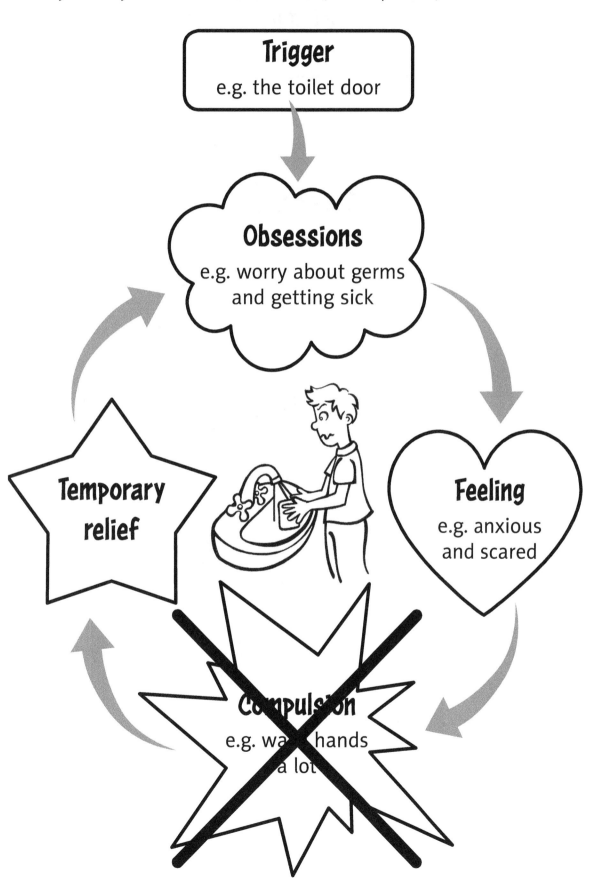

Complete some more OCD cycles to help you (you and us all) to really understand how your OCD works.

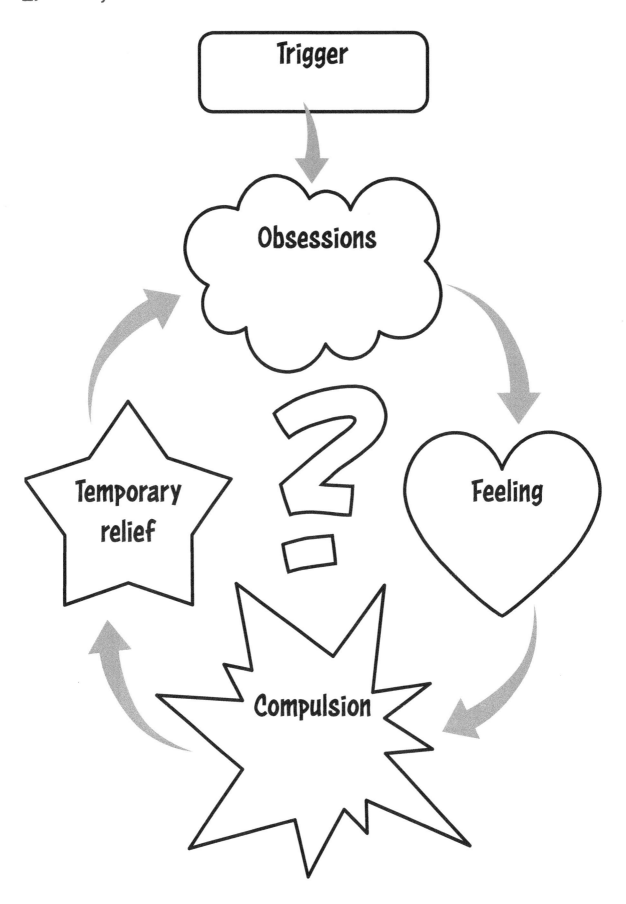

Trigger

Obsessions

Temporary relief

Feeling

Compulsion

Complete some more OCD cycles to help you (you and us all) to really understand how your OCD works.

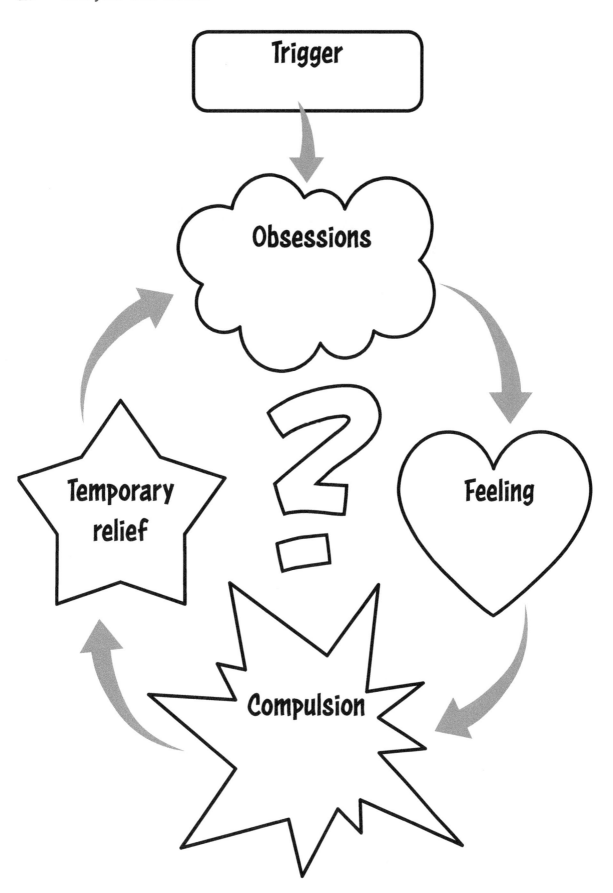

Complete some more OCD cycles to help you (you and us all) to really understand how your OCD works.

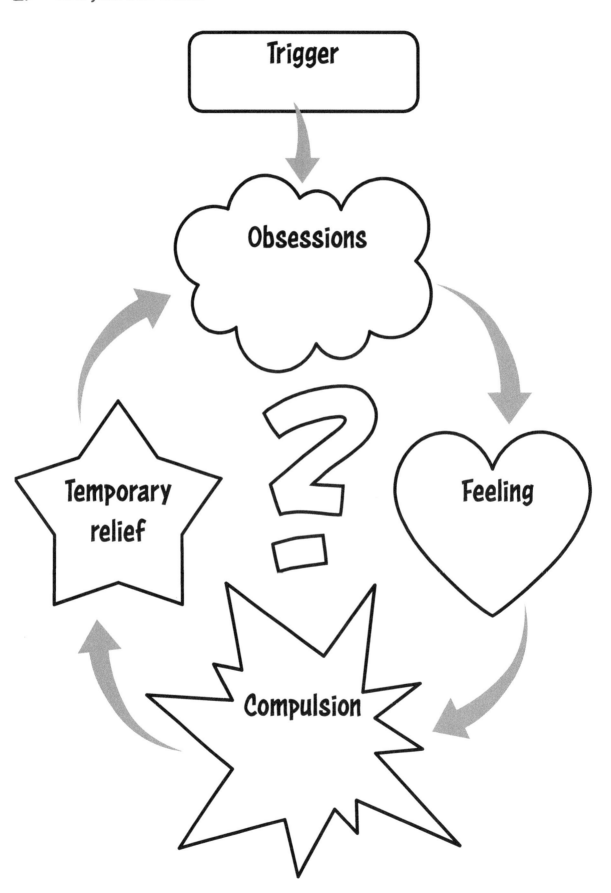

WHAT IS CBT?

■ CBT stands for cognitive behaviour therapy.

■ This just means a treatment that works with your thoughts (cognitions) and your behaviours.

■ The main tool we will learn in CBT is called **'exposure and response prevention'** or **ERP** for short.

■ **Exposure** means **'facing the fear'**. OCD makes us feel scared or uncomfortable a lot of the time and 'tricks' us into worrying or doing silly things. When we 'face the fear', we start to do the things that OCD makes us feel frightened of and we learn that OCD is really nothing to be afraid of!

■ **Response prevention** means **'fighting the action'**. When we face the OCD worry, or do what we feel frightened of doing, we need to make sure that we do *not* do any compulsions or take any action to make the worry go away.

■ ERP or 'facing the fear' and 'fighting the action' might seem like a scary thing to do, but your therapist will help you and you will never be asked to do anything that you do not feel ready to do. We will always go at your pace and we will fight back against the OCD using small steps!

■ We will also learn some other 'thinking tools' to use when OCD tries to trick us into worrying about things.

GOALS

Consider some goals for therapy. They should be **S**pecific, **M**easurable, **A**chievable, **R**ealistic and **T**imed – SMART! Ask your therapist about SMART goals.

Imagine you woke up tomorrow morning and your OCD was gone. What would you be able to do that you are not doing now?

By the middle of treatment, I would like to be able to:

1. _____

2. _____

3. _____

By the end of treatment, I would like to be able to:

1. _____

2. _____

3. _____

Bigger things I will be able to do if I achieve my goals above include:

1. _____

2. _____

3. _____

HOMEWORK: SESSION 2

- Read over Session 2.

- Complete the OCD hierarchy.

- Complete the goals sheet.

- Complete some more OCD cycle sheets.

- Other homework:

_____

_____

_____

_____

_____

_____

_____

- Write three things you learned/will remember from Session 2:

_____

_____

_____

_____

- Write any questions here that you want to ask next time. Is there anything you want to know or learn more about?

_____

_____

_____

_____

_____

TOOLS FOR FIGHTING OCD

Recap: What have you learned so far?

In your first two sessions, you have learned the following tools for fighting OCD:

- **Tool 1:** Externalising OCD
- **Tool 2:** Understanding anxiety by recognising how anxiety feels in your body, rating anxiety on a 1–10 scale and knowing that anxiety comes down over time
- **Tool 3:** Making an OCD hierarchy
- **Tool 4:** The OCD cycle.

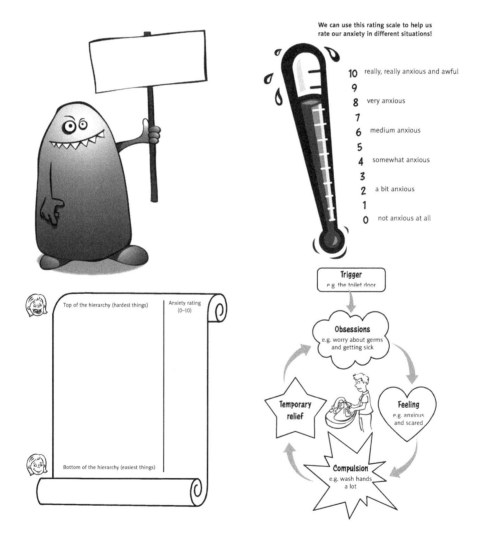

In Session 3 you will learn:

- **Tool 5:** Our first exposure and response prevention (ERP) task – this is where you really start fighting OCD!
- **Tool 6:** Bossing back OCD using helpful thoughts.

Tools for fighting OCD

TOOL 5: OUR FIRST ERP TASK

Tips for choosing the first ERP task:

- You could choose something that you already resist from time to time.

- Some people choose the things that they find the most annoying.

- Choose something that you feel confident you can achieve but that is not too easy – maybe a 4 or 5 on your anxiety scale.

STEP 1 Let's pick one thing that OCD makes you do (you can use the OCD list to help you).
- What is it OCD makes you do and why do you do this? (What is the fear or obsession?)

_____

STEP 2 What is your fighting back task going to be?

_____

STEP 3 Rate how scared or worried you feel about **NOT** doing the thing that OCD wants you to do (use the rating scale **0–10**).

_____

STEP 4 Do you need anyone or anything to help you?

_____

STEP 5 Face the fear and fight the action! **Do what OCD is trying to tell you _not_ to do!**

STEP 6 Well done! Now let's record your feelings of anxiety. Use the table on the next page to help you. Remember to rate how scared or worried you feel using the rating scale (**0–10**).

STEP 7 Rate your feelings of anxiety every few minutes until it comes right down.

STEP 8 What have you learned from this task?
- What have you learned about your anxiety?
- What does this task tell you about the fear or worry you identified in Step 1 (the obsession)?

_____

STEP 9 You have won this battle with OCD! How will you reward yourself for the hard work?

WELL DONE!

Fight back against the OCD. Let's see what happens to your anxiety when you do this.

Date	Your ERP fighting back task is?	Anxiety ratings				
		0 min	5 min	15 min	30 min	1 hr

You have measured your anxiety over one hour. Consider what happens to it after two, three, four hours, overnight or by the next day. For your exposure task to be useful, keep recording your anxiety until it has come down at least by half (e.g. from 6 to 3).

Tools for fighting OCD

TOOL 6: BOSSING BACK OCD USING HELPFUL THOUGHTS

- OCD likes to try and trick the way you think by making you believe in the OCD thoughts.

- When you fight OCD, it is useful to practise thinking in HELPFUL WAYS!

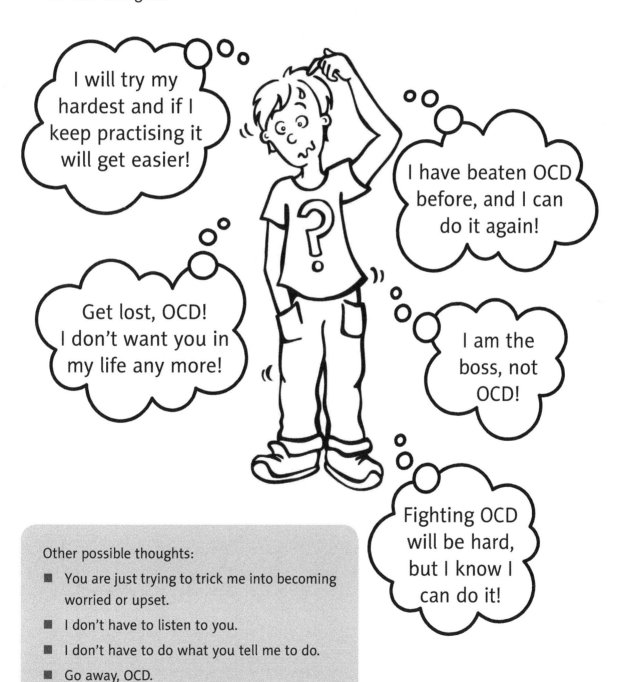

Other possible thoughts:

- You are just trying to trick me into becoming worried or upset.
- I don't have to listen to you.
- I don't have to do what you tell me to do.
- Go away, OCD.
- I'm not going to do what you want any more.

45

Thinking helpful thoughts can help us to feel confident in fighting back against the OCD.

What helpful thoughts can you use?

Warning! Be careful not to give yourself reassurance. To learn more about reassurance in OCD, go to Tool 8 on page 112.

FIGHTING BACK: USING ERP TO BEAT OCD

STEP 1 Let's pick one thing that OCD makes you do (you can use the OCD list to help you).

- What is it OCD makes you do and why do you do this? (What is the fear or obsession?)

_____

_____

_____

STEP 2 What is your fighting back task going to be?

_____

_____

_____

STEP 3 Rate how scared or worried you feel about **NOT** doing the thing that OCD wants you to do (use the rating scale **0–10**).

_____

_____

STEP 4 Do you need anyone or anything to help you? Don't forget to use your helpful thoughts!

_____

_____

STEP 5 Face the fear and fight the action! **Do what OCD is trying to tell you *not* to do!**

STEP 6 Well done! Now let's record your feelings of anxiety. Use the table on the next page to help you. Remember to rate how scared or worried you feel using the rating scale (**0–10**).

STEP 7 Don't forget to keep fighting back against the OCD by using helpful thoughts.

STEP 8 Rate your feelings of anxiety every few minutes until it comes right down.

STEP 9 What have you learned from this task?

- What have you learned about your anxiety?
- What does this task tell you about the fear or worry you identified in Step 1 (the obsession)?

_____

_____

STEP 10 You have won this battle with OCD! How will you reward yourself for the hard work?

WELL DONE!

Fight back against the OCD. Let's see what happens to your anxiety when you do this.

Date	Your ERP fighting back task is?	Anxiety ratings				
		0 min	5 min	15 min	30 min	1 hr

You have measured your anxiety over one hour. Consider what happens to it after two, three, four hours, overnight or by the next day. For your exposure task to be useful, keep recording your anxiety until it has come down at least by half (e.g. from 6 to 3).

HOMEWORK: SESSION 3

■ What fighting back task(s) are you going to practise this week?

_____

_____

_____

_____

■ Additional things to work on this week:

_____

_____

_____

_____

■ Three things you learned/will remember from Session 3:

_____

_____

_____

_____

■ Write any questions here that you want to ask next time:

_____

_____

_____

_____

FIGHTING BACK: SESSION 4

STEP 1 Let's pick one thing that OCD makes you do (you can use the OCD list to help you).

■ What is it OCD makes you do and why do you do this? (What is the fear or obsession?)

_____

_____

_____

STEP 2 What is your fighting back task going to be?

_____

_____

_____

STEP 3 Rate how scared or worried you feel about **NOT** doing the thing that OCD wants you to do (use the rating scale **0–10**).

_____

_____

STEP 4 Do you need anyone or anything to help you? Don't forget to use your helpful thoughts!

_____

_____

STEP 5 Face the fear and fight the action! **Do what OCD is trying to tell you _not_ to do!**

STEP 6 Well done! Now let's record your feelings of anxiety. Use the table on the next page to help you. Remember to rate how scared or worried you feel using the rating scale (**0–10**).

STEP 7 Don't forget to keep fighting back against the OCD by using helpful thoughts.

STEP 8 Rate your feelings of anxiety every few minutes until it comes right down.

STEP 9 What have you learned from this task?

■ What have you learned about your anxiety?

■ What does this task tell you about the fear or worry you identified in Step 1 (the obsession)?

_____

_____

STEP 10 You have won this battle with OCD! How will you reward yourself for the hard work?

WELL DONE!

Fight back against the OCD. Let's see what happens to your anxiety when you do this.

Date	Your ERP fighting back task is?	Anxiety ratings				
		0 min	5 min	15 min	30 min	1 hr

You have measured your anxiety over one hour. Consider what happens to it after two, three, four hours, overnight or by the next day. For your exposure task to be useful, keep recording your anxiety until it has come down at least by half (e.g. from 6 to 3).

FIGHTING BACK: SESSION 4

Sometimes tasks feel too big to tackle in one go. Use this sheet to break the task down into manageable steps.

HOMEWORK: SESSION 4

■ What fighting back task(s) are you going to practise this week?

_____

_____

_____

_____

_____

_____

■ Additional things to work on this week:

_____

_____

_____

_____

_____

_____

■ Write any questions here that you want to ask next time:

_____

_____

_____

_____

_____

_____

FIGHTING BACK: SESSION 5

STEP 1 Let's pick one thing that OCD makes you do (you can use the OCD list to help you).
- What is it OCD makes you do and why do you do this? (What is the fear or obsession?)

_____

_____

_____

STEP 2 What is your fighting back task going to be?

_____

_____

_____

STEP 3 Rate how scared or worried you feel about **NOT** doing the thing that OCD wants you to do (use the rating scale **0–10**).

_____

_____

STEP 4 Do you need anyone or anything to help you? Don't forget to use your helpful thoughts!

_____

_____

STEP 5 Face the fear and fight the action! **Do what OCD is trying to tell you _not_ to do!**

STEP 6 Well done! Now let's record your feelings of anxiety. Use the table on the next page to help you. Remember to rate how scared or worried you feel using the rating scale (**0–10**).

STEP 7 Don't forget to keep fighting back against the OCD by using helpful thoughts.

STEP 8 Rate your feelings of anxiety every few minutes until it comes right down.

STEP 9 What have you learned from this task?
- What have you learned about your anxiety?
- What does this task tell you about the fear or worry you identified in Step 1 (the obsession)?

_____

_____

STEP 10 You have won this battle with OCD! How will you reward yourself for the hard work?

WELL DONE!

Fight back against the OCD. Let's see what happens to your anxiety when you do this.

Date	Your ERP fighting back task is?	Anxiety ratings				
		0 min	5 min	15 min	30 min	1 hr

You have measured your anxiety over one hour. Consider what happens to it after two, three, four hours, overnight or by the next day. For your exposure task to be useful, keep recording your anxiety until it has come down at least by half (e.g. from 6 to 3).

FIGHTING BACK: SESSION 5

Sometimes tasks feel too big to tackle in one go. Use this sheet to break the task down into manageable steps.

HOMEWORK: SESSION 5

- What fighting back task(s) are you going to practise this week?

_____

_____

_____

_____

_____

_____

- Additional things to work on this week:

_____

_____

_____

_____

_____

_____

- Write any questions here that you want to ask next time:

_____

_____

_____

_____

_____

_____

FIGHTING BACK: SESSION 6

STEP 1 Let's pick one thing that OCD makes you do (you can use the OCD list to help you).

- What is it OCD makes you do and why do you do this? (What is the fear or obsession?)

_____

_____

_____

STEP 2 What is your fighting back task going to be?

_____

_____

_____

STEP 3 Rate how scared or worried you feel about **NOT** doing the thing that OCD wants you to do (use the rating scale **0–10**).

_____

_____

STEP 4 Do you need anyone or anything to help you? Don't forget to use your helpful thoughts!

_____

_____

STEP 5 Face the fear and fight the action! **Do what OCD is trying to tell you *not* to do!**

STEP 6 Well done! Now let's record your feelings of anxiety. Use the table on the next page to help you. Remember to rate how scared or worried you feel using the rating scale (**0–10**).

STEP 7 Don't forget to keep fighting back against the OCD by using helpful thoughts.

STEP 8 Rate your feelings of anxiety every few minutes until it comes right down.

STEP 9 What have you learned from this task?

- What have you learned about your anxiety?
- What does this task tell you about the fear or worry you identified in Step 1 (the obsession)?

_____

_____

STEP 10 You have won this battle with OCD! How will you reward yourself for the hard work?

WELL DONE!

Fight back against the OCD. Let's see what happens to your anxiety when you do this.

Date	Your ERP fighting back task is?	Anxiety ratings				
		0 min	5 min	15 min	30 min	1 hr

You have measured your anxiety over one hour. Consider what happens to it after two, three, four hours, overnight or by the next day. For your exposure task to be useful, keep recording your anxiety until it has come down at least by half (e.g. from 6 to 3).

Sometimes tasks feel too big to tackle in one go. Use this sheet to break the task down into manageable steps.

HOMEWORK: SESSION 6

- What fighting back task(s) are you going to practise this week?

  _____

  _____

  _____

  _____

  _____

- Additional things to work on this week:

  _____

  _____

  _____

  _____

  _____

- Write any questions here that you want to ask next time:

  _____

  _____

  _____

  _____

  _____

LET'S REVIEW AND MEASURE YOUR OCD AGAIN

■ We know how sneaky and secretive OCD is, so it is important to keep looking at it and measuring it to make sure you are making progress with your fight against it.

■ Your therapist will measure your OCD at this session or may give you a questionnaire to take home. This is a really good way to track your progress in fighting OCD.

■ Record your progress here:

- Score/level of severity at start of treatment (date):

_____

_____

_____

- Score/level of severity mid-treatment (date):

_____

_____

_____

RE-RATE YOUR OCD HIERARCHY

- It's helpful to use the OCD hierarchy to see just how well you are doing in your fight against OCD.

- Take some time to re-rate how anxious you would feel now if you were to resist doing what OCD wanted you to do.

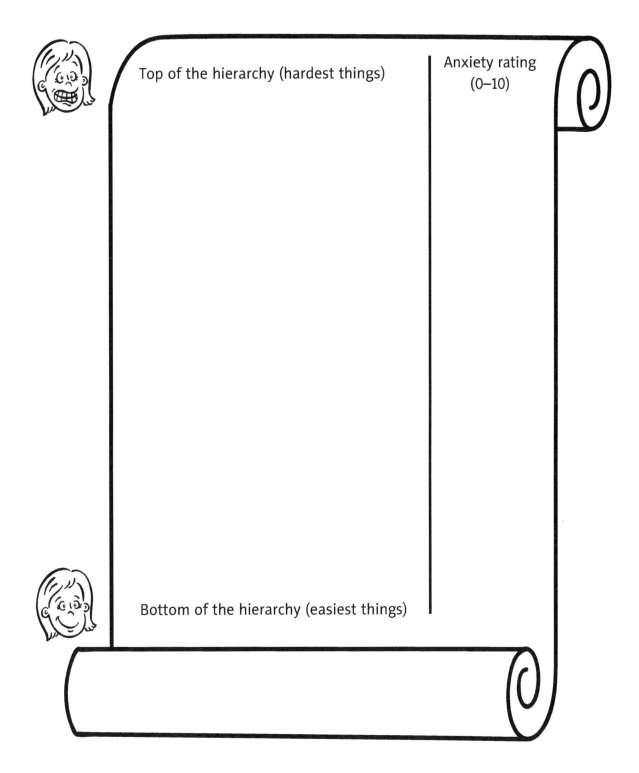

Top of the hierarchy (hardest things)

Anxiety rating (0–10)

Bottom of the hierarchy (easiest things)

FIGHTING BACK: SESSION 7

STEP 1 Let's pick one thing that OCD makes you do (you can use the OCD list to help you).

- What is it OCD makes you do and why do you do this? (What is the fear or obsession?)

_____

_____

_____

STEP 2 What is your fighting back task going to be?

_____

_____

_____

STEP 3 Rate how scared or worried you feel about **NOT** doing the thing that OCD wants you to do (use the rating scale **0–10**).

_____

_____

STEP 4 Do you need anyone or anything to help you? Don't forget to use your helpful thoughts!

_____

_____

STEP 5 Face the fear and fight the action! **Do what OCD is trying to tell you _not_ to do!**

STEP 6 Well done! Now let's record your feelings of anxiety. Use the table on the next page to help you. Remember to rate how scared or worried you feel using the rating scale (**0–10**).

STEP 7 Don't forget to keep fighting back against the OCD by using helpful thoughts.

STEP 8 Rate your feelings of anxiety every few minutes until it comes right down.

STEP 9 What have you learned from this task?

- What have you learned about your anxiety?
- What does this task tell you about the fear or worry you identified in Step 1 (the obsession)?

_____

_____

STEP 10 You have won this battle with OCD! How will you reward yourself for the hard work?

WELL DONE!

Fight back against the OCD. Let's see what happens to your anxiety when you do this.

Date	Your ERP fighting back task is?	Anxiety ratings				
		0 min	5 min	15 min	30 min	1 hr

You have measured your anxiety over one hour. Consider what happens to it after two, three, four hours, overnight or by the next day. For your exposure task to be useful, keep recording your anxiety until it has come down at least by half (e.g. from 6 to 3).

Sometimes tasks feel too big to tackle in one go. Use this sheet to break the task down into manageable steps.

HOMEWORK: SESSION 7

■ What fighting back task(s) are you going to practise this week?

_____

_____

_____

_____

_____

_____

■ Additional things to work on this week:

_____

_____

_____

_____

_____

_____

■ Write any questions here that you want to ask next time.

_____

_____

_____

_____

_____

_____

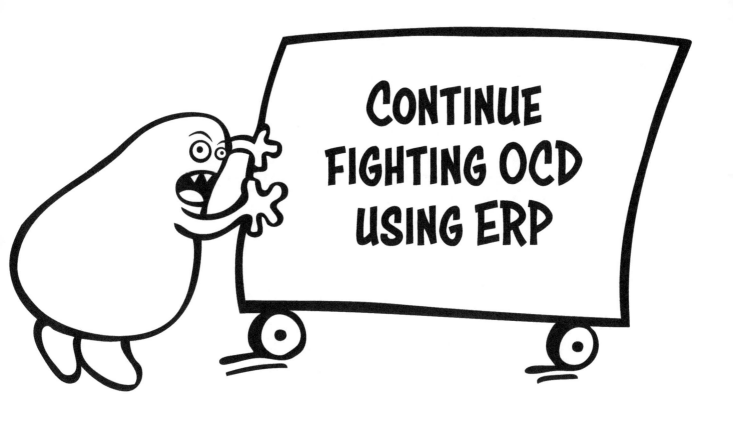

FIGHTING BACK: SESSION 8

STEP 1 Let's pick one thing that OCD makes you do (you can use the OCD list to help you).

- What is it OCD makes you do and why do you do this? (What is the fear or obsession?)

_____

_____

_____

STEP 2 What is your fighting back task going to be?

_____

_____

_____

STEP 3 Rate how scared or worried you feel about **NOT** doing the thing that OCD wants you to do (use the rating scale **0–10**).

_____

_____

STEP 4 Do you need anyone or anything to help you? Don't forget to use your helpful thoughts!

_____

_____

STEP 5 Face the fear and fight the action! **Do what OCD is trying to tell you _not_ to do!**

STEP 6 Well done! Now let's record your feelings of anxiety. Use the table on the next page to help you. Remember to rate how scared or worried you feel using the rating scale (**0–10**).

STEP 7 Don't forget to keep fighting back against the OCD by using helpful thoughts.

STEP 8 Rate your feelings of anxiety every few minutes until it comes right down.

STEP 9 What have you learned from this task?

- What have you learned about your anxiety?
- What does this task tell you about the fear or worry you identified in Step 1 (the obsession)?

_____

_____

STEP 10 You have won this battle with OCD! How will you reward yourself for the hard work?

WELL DONE!

Fight back against the OCD. Let's see what happens to your anxiety when you do this.

Date	Your ERP fighting back task is?	Anxiety ratings				
		0 min	5 min	15 min	30 min	1 hr

You have measured your anxiety over one hour. Consider what happens to it after two, three, four hours, overnight or by the next day. For your exposure task to be useful, keep recording your anxiety until it has come down at least by half (e.g. from 6 to 3).

Sometimes tasks feel too big to tackle in one go. Use this sheet to break the task down into manageable steps.

Homework: Session 8

■ What fighting back task(s) are you going to practise this week?

_____

_____

_____

_____

_____

_____

■ Additional things to work on this week:

_____

_____

_____

_____

_____

_____

■ Write any questions here that you want to ask next time:

_____

_____

_____

_____

_____

_____

FIGHTING BACK: SESSION 9

STEP 1 Let's pick one thing that OCD makes you do (you can use the OCD list to help you).

- What is it OCD makes you do and why do you do this? (What is the fear or obsession?)

_____

_____

_____

STEP 2 What is your fighting back task going to be?

_____

_____

_____

STEP 3 Rate how scared or worried you feel about **NOT** doing the thing that OCD wants you to do (use the rating scale **0–10**).

_____

_____

STEP 4 Do you need anyone or anything to help you? Don't forget to use your helpful thoughts!

_____

_____

STEP 5 Face the fear and fight the action! **Do what OCD is trying to tell you _not_ to do!**

STEP 6 Well done! Now let's record your feelings of anxiety. Use the table on the next page to help you. Remember to rate how scared or worried you feel using the rating scale (**0–10**).

STEP 7 Don't forget to keep fighting back against the OCD by using helpful thoughts.

STEP 8 Rate your feelings of anxiety every few minutes until it comes right down.

STEP 9 What have you learned from this task?

- What have you learned about your anxiety?
- What does this task tell you about the fear or worry you identified in Step 1 (the obsession)?

_____

_____

STEP 10 You have won this battle with OCD! How will you reward yourself for the hard work?

WELL DONE!

Fight back against the OCD. Let's see what happens to your anxiety when you do this.

Date	Your ERP fighting back task is?	Anxiety ratings				
		0 min	5 min	15 min	30 min	1 hr

You have measured your anxiety over one hour. Consider what happens to it after two, three, four hours, overnight or by the next day. For your exposure task to be useful, keep recording your anxiety until it has come down at least by half (e.g. from 6 to 3).

🖊 Sometimes tasks feel too big to tackle in one go. Use this sheet to break the task down into manageable steps.

HOMEWORK: SESSION 9

■ What fighting back task(s) are you going to practise this week?

_____

_____

_____

_____

_____

_____

■ Additional things to work on this week:

_____

_____

_____

_____

_____

_____

■ Write any questions here that you want to ask next time:

_____

_____

_____

_____

_____

_____

Fighting Back: Session 10

STEP 1 Let's pick one thing that OCD makes you do (you can use the OCD list to help you).

■ What is it OCD makes you do and why do you do this? (What is the fear or obsession?)

_____

_____

_____

STEP 2 What is your fighting back task going to be?

_____

_____

_____

STEP 3 Rate how scared or worried you feel about **NOT** doing the thing that OCD wants you to do (use the rating scale **0–10**).

_____

_____

STEP 4 Do you need anyone or anything to help you? Don't forget to use your helpful thoughts!

_____

_____

STEP 5 Face the fear and fight the action! **Do what OCD is trying to tell you _not_ to do!**

STEP 6 Well done! Now let's record your feelings of anxiety. Use the table on the next page to help you. Remember to rate how scared or worried you feel using the rating scale (**0–10**).

STEP 7 Don't forget to keep fighting back against the OCD by using helpful thoughts.

STEP 8 Rate your feelings of anxiety every few minutes until it comes right down.

STEP 9 What have you learned from this task?

■ What have you learned about your anxiety?

■ What does this task tell you about the fear or worry you identified in Step 1 (the obsession)?

_____

_____

STEP 10 You have won this battle with OCD! How will you reward yourself for the hard work?

WELL DONE!

Fight back against the OCD. Let's see what happens to your anxiety when you do this.

Date	Your ERP fighting back task is?	Anxiety ratings				
		0 min	5 min	15 min	30 min	1 hr

You have measured your anxiety over one hour. Consider what happens to it after two, three, four hours, overnight or by the next day. For your exposure task to be useful, keep recording your anxiety until it has come down at least by half (e.g. from 6 to 3).

Sometimes tasks feel too big to tackle in one go. Use this sheet to break the task down into manageable steps.

Homework: Session 10

■ What fighting back task(s) are you going to practise this week?

_____

_____

_____

_____

_____

_____

■ Additional things to work on this week:

_____

_____

_____

_____

_____

_____

■ Write any questions here that you want to ask next time:

_____

_____

_____

_____

_____

_____

FIGHTING BACK: SESSION 11

STEP 1 Let's pick one thing that OCD makes you do (you can use the OCD list to help you).

■ What is it OCD makes you do and why do you do this? (What is the fear or obsession?)

_____

_____

_____

STEP 2 What is your fighting back task going to be?

_____

_____

_____

STEP 3 Rate how scared or worried you feel about **NOT** doing the thing that OCD wants you to do (use the rating scale **0–10**).

_____

_____

STEP 4 Do you need anyone or anything to help you? Don't forget to use your helpful thoughts!

_____

_____

STEP 5 Face the fear and fight the action! **Do what OCD is trying to tell you _not_ to do!**

STEP 6 Well done! Now let's record your feelings of anxiety. Use the table on the next page to help you. Remember to rate how scared or worried you feel using the rating scale (**0–10**).

STEP 7 Don't forget to keep fighting back against the OCD by using helpful thoughts.

STEP 8 Rate your feelings of anxiety every few minutes until it comes right down.

STEP 9 What have you learned from this task?

■ What have you learned about your anxiety?

■ What does this task tell you about the fear or worry you identified in Step 1 (the obsession)?

_____

_____

STEP 10 You have won this battle with OCD! How will you reward yourself for the hard work?

WELL DONE!

Fight back against the OCD. Let's see what happens to your anxiety when you do this.

Date	Your ERP fighting back task is?	Anxiety ratings				
		0 min	5 min	15 min	30 min	1 hr

You have measured your anxiety over one hour. Consider what happens to it after two, three, four hours, overnight or by the next day. For your exposure task to be useful, keep recording your anxiety until it has come down at least by half (e.g. from 6 to 3).

Sometimes tasks feel too big to tackle in one go. Use this sheet to break the task down into manageable steps.

HOMEWORK: SESSION 11

■ What fighting back task(s) are you going to practise this week?

_____

_____

_____

_____

_____

_____

■ Additional things to work on this week:

_____

_____

_____

_____

_____

_____

■ Write any questions here that you want to ask next time:

_____

_____

_____

_____

_____

_____

FIGHTING BACK: SESSION 12

STEP 1 Let's pick one thing that OCD makes you do (you can use the OCD list to help you).

- What is it OCD makes you do and why do you do this? (What is the fear or obsession?)

_____

_____

_____

STEP 2 What is your fighting back task going to be?

_____

_____

_____

STEP 3 Rate how scared or worried you feel about **NOT** doing the thing that OCD wants you to do (use the rating scale **0–10**).

_____

_____

STEP 4 Do you need anyone or anything to help you? Don't forget to use your helpful thoughts!

_____

_____

STEP 5 Face the fear and fight the action! **Do what OCD is trying to tell you *not* to do!**

STEP 6 Well done! Now let's record your feelings of anxiety. Use the table on the next page to help you. Remember to rate how scared or worried you feel using the rating scale (**0–10**).

STEP 7 Don't forget to keep fighting back against the OCD by using helpful thoughts.

STEP 8 Rate your feelings of anxiety every few minutes until it comes right down.

STEP 9 What have you learned from this task?

- What have you learned about your anxiety?
- What does this task tell you about the fear or worry you identified in Step 1 (the obsession)?

_____

_____

STEP 10 You have won this battle with OCD! How will you reward yourself for the hard work?

WELL DONE!

Fight back against the OCD. Let's see what happens to your anxiety when you do this.

Date	Your ERP fighting back task is?	Anxiety ratings				
		0 min	5 min	15 min	30 min	1 hr

You have measured your anxiety over one hour. Consider what happens to it after two, three, four hours, overnight or by the next day. For your exposure task to be useful, keep recording your anxiety until it has come down at least by half (e.g. from 6 to 3).

FIGHTING BACK: SESSION 12

Sometimes tasks feel too big to tackle in one go. Use this sheet to break the task down into manageable steps.

HOMEWORK: SESSION 12

■ What fighting back task(s) are you going to practise this week?

_____

_____

_____

_____

_____

■ Additional things to work on this week:

_____

_____

_____

_____

_____

_____

■ Write any questions here that you want to ask next time:

_____

_____

_____

_____

_____

_____

TAKE IT TO THE EXTREME - OVERLEARNING IN OCD!

- Once you feel as if you have tackled most of your compulsions, it is tempting to think 'this is good enough'. However, to make sure that you have truly beaten OCD once and for all, it is helpful to do an overlearning task.

- This is your way of proving that OCD does not have any control over you any more.

- Unlike regular ERP tasks, this overlearning task is not something that you would practise every day. It might be something that you just do once, as proof of your victory over OCD.

- For example, if OCD makes you worry about toilet germs, how about you place a piece of food on a toilet seat and then eat it? Not something you would do every day but I think you would agree you have triumphed over OCD if you could do this!

- Or let's say OCD makes you worry about making a mistake in your school work, perhaps you could deliberately make a big error in a piece of school work and hand it in without explaining to your teacher – again, not something you would keep repeating!

- Sometimes an overlearning task involves **taking a risk** and/or **tolerating uncertainty**. These are two very important things to master if you want to stay well away from OCD.

- What could your overlearning task be? Talk it over with your therapist. Design your task below:

_____

_____

_____

_____

_____

_____

_____

Don't forget to do your regular ERP task in the session too, and plan for homework!

FIGHTING BACK: SESSION 13

STEP 1 Let's pick one thing that OCD makes you do (you can use the OCD list to help you).

- What is it OCD makes you do and why do you do this? (What is the fear or obsession?)

_____

_____

_____

STEP 2 What is your overlearning back task going to be?

_____

_____

_____

STEP 3 Rate how scared or worried you feel about **NOT** doing the thing that OCD wants you to do (use the rating scale **0–10**).

_____

_____

STEP 4 Do you need anyone or anything to help you? Don't forget to use your helpful thoughts!

_____

_____

STEP 5 Face the fear and fight the action! **Do what OCD is trying to tell you *not* to do!**

STEP 6 Well done! Now let's record your feelings of anxiety. Use the table on the next page to help you. Remember to rate how scared or worried you feel using the rating scale (**0–10**).

STEP 7 Don't forget to keep fighting back against the OCD by using helpful thoughts.

STEP 8 Rate your feelings of anxiety every few minutes until it comes right down.

STEP 9 What have you learned from this task?

- What have you learned about your anxiety?
- What does this task tell you about the fear or worry you identified in Step 1 (the obsession)?

_____

_____

STEP 10 You have won this battle with OCD! How will you reward yourself for the hard work?

WELL DONE!

Fight back against the OCD. Let's see what happens to your anxiety when you do this.

Date	Your ERP fighting back task is?	Anxiety ratings				
		0 min	5 min	15 min	30 min	1 hr

You have measured your anxiety over one hour. Consider what happens to it after two, three, four hours, overnight or by the next day. For your exposure task to be useful, keep recording your anxiety until it has come down at least by half (e.g. from 6 to 3).

Sometimes tasks feel too big to tackle in one go. Use this sheet to break the task down into manageable steps.

HOMEWORK: SESSION 13

■ What is your overlearning task going to be?

_____

_____

_____

_____

■ What fighting back task(s) are you going to practise this week?

_____

_____

_____

_____

■ Additional things to work on this week:

_____

_____

_____

_____

■ Write any questions here that you want to ask next time:

_____

_____

_____

_____

LET'S REVIEW AND MEASURE YOUR OCD AGAIN

■ We know how sneaky and secretive OCD is, so it is important to keep looking at it and measuring it to make sure you are making progress with your fight against it.

■ Your therapist will measure your OCD at this session or may give you a questionnaire to take home. This is a really good way to track your progress in fighting OCD.

■ Record your progress here:

• Score/level of severity at start of treatment (date):

_____

_____

_____

• Score/level of severity mid-treatment (date):

_____

_____

_____

• Score/level of severity at end of treatment (date):

_____

_____

_____

RELAPSE PREVENTION

What have you learned about fighting OCD?

The best way to keep hold of the gains you have made in your treatment is to keep going and to remember what you learned in CBT. To help you think about this ask yourself the following questions: How did my OCD start? What kept it going? What did I learn in therapy? What strategies have I learned that I wouldn't want to ever forget? What are my goals for the future? What will help me to achieve these goals?

Write down the five most important things you learned in CBT:

1. _____

_____

2. _____

_____

3. _____

_____

4. _____

_____

5. _____

_____

_____

_____

_____

_____

_____

_____

_____

_____

RELAPSE PREVENTION CONTINUED

Keep fighting back!

- Your CBT sessions are coming to an end but that does not mean the end of fighting OCD! Most people have some OCD symptoms left at the end of treatment.

- The good news is that you are now an expert in fighting OCD and you can keep fighting OCD – you can be your own therapist.

- Let's plan what you are going to fight over the next month. Think about the compulsions that OCD is still making you do, or things you are still avoiding because of OCD.

- What will your ERP tasks be?

_____

_____

_____

_____

_____

_____

_____

_____

_____

_____

Fantastic! Although you won't be seeing your therapist as much any more, you are not on your own.

Remember that you can win against OCD. Use all the tools you have been taught to keep OCD out of your life.

Relapse Prevention Continued

If OCD tries to come back, be prepared!
When might it come back?

- If OCD does try to get back into your life, it might try and do so at a time when you are feeling stressed or worried about other things.

- Try to think of what events or things might be coming up in your life that could be a little bit stressful (e.g. changing school, exams, moving house, arguments or disagreements with friends or family members).

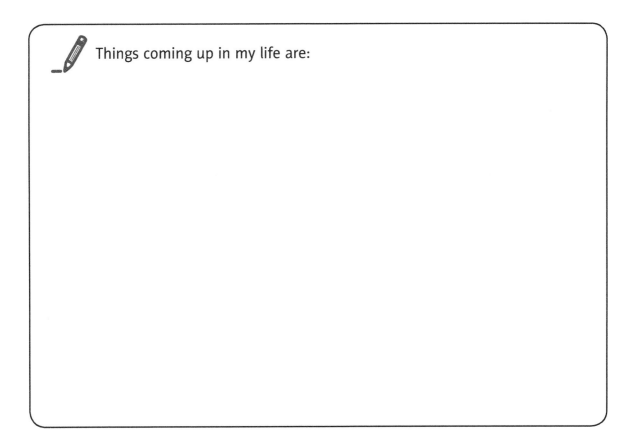

Things coming up in my life are:

- ## What sort of symptoms?

What sort of OCD symptoms might be most likely to return?

_____

_____

_____

_____

_____

_____

_____

_____

_____

_____

- ## Who would notice if OCD started creeping back?

_____

- ## Tell someone!

OCD likes to be kept a secret! Another trick OCD uses is to keep itself a secret. You have already beaten this, because you have told your family, and you have come for help. If OCD does try to come back, make sure you tell someone before it becomes a problem!!

- ## Act early!

Don't avoid doing anything about it. OCD is easiest to fight when it is caught early. If you start to fight it right away, it is unlikely that the OCD will gain control. So let's make a relapse prevention plan!

Tools for fighting OCD

TOOL 7: A RELAPSE PREVENTION PLAN

■ It's important to feel prepared just in case OCD does try to come back.

■ In the space below, you can write your plan for what you would do if OCD started to bother you again. What are the golden rules for fighting OCD?

■ It is easier to fight OCD when you are not alone. Think of who could help you. How might they help you?

 Use this space to note down your relapse prevention plan.

TOOL 7: A RELAPSE PREVENTION PLAN CONTINUED

My life

Another important part of recovery from OCD and relapse prevention is building up the non-OCD aspects of your life.

■ What things are you looking forward to being able to do without OCD interfering so much in your life?

_____

_____

_____

_____

■ Try to think of some life goals. What would you like to do now, and in the future?

_____

_____

_____

_____

■ What will help you to achieve these goals?

_____

_____

_____

_____

_____

_____

_____

ADDITIONAL TOOLS FOR FIGHTING OCD

Tools for fighting OCD

Tool 8: Reassurance seeking and accommodation of OCD

Reassurance seeking

- Reassurance seeking is when OCD makes you ask questions to try to reduce your anxiety.

- Reassurance seeking is very much like a compulsion, and therefore it should be tackled in just the same way by using ERP.

- There are lots of comments and actions from our family and friends that can give reassurance. Although these things can bring down your level of anxiety and make you feel better, that relief from anxiety is temporary! Reassurance can accidentally make OCD stronger. Our aim in treatment of OCD is to encourage you to **tolerate** the anxiety, **not to help bring it down with reassurance.**

- Often OCD can make you ask for reassurance in quite subtle ways.

What does reassurance seeking look like for you?

List the type of questions that OCD prompts you to ask your friends and family in order to get reassurance.

_____

_____

_____

_____

_____

Some common ways that family and friends might offer you reassurance are to say things like:

- Don't worry. It'll be okay.

- It's fine, I'm sure it's clean.

- Nothing bad is going to happen.

- Of course you won't get sick.

It's important that your family and friends **learn new ways of responding** to OCD instead of reassurance seeking.

> What could they say instead?
>
> - If possible, try and ignore the question/comment completely and redirect to a new topic/activity. (They are ignoring the comment, but not ignoring you.)
>
> - If they have to reply, they could say:
>
>   - 'I can't answer that, it's an OCD question/comment.'
>
>   - 'You're doing well fighting OCD.'
>
> - Once you have achieved this, you could set up an ERP task where your family/friends practise saying the opposite of what OCD would like, for example, 'Maybe something bad will happen to us, maybe we are not safe?'

Accommodation of (or doing things for) OCD

What does OCD get your family and friends to do? Examples of things that family and friends often find themselves doing for OCD include:

- assisting in washing and cleaning rituals

- having to say/repeat things in certain ways

- avoiding touching things

- giving reassurance (as discussed above).

As treatment progresses, you will ask your family and friends **not** to do any of these things for OCD.

> What can they do instead?
>
> - Your family's accommodation of OCD should be included on your hierarchy with the question 'How anxious would it make you feel if they did not do X?'
>
> - Then accommodation should be tackled like any other compulsion, i.e. set up a deliberate trigger for this accommodation, then your family member deliberately resists doing it – you monitor the anxiety that results from this. Repeat the practice daily until the anxiety comes down.

Tools for fighting OCD

Tool 9: Normalising intrusive thoughts

Intrusive thoughts are normal

- Everyone has weird, scary, inappropriate and rude thoughts popping into their head from time to time.

- In fact, research shows that people *without* OCD have exactly the same types of thoughts as people *with* OCD. The only difference is that people without OCD tend to shrug them off quite easily. They might think to themselves, 'That was a weird thought...oh well' and then get on with their day, or they might even laugh about it. As you probably already know, OCD usually makes people very upset about intrusive thoughts. You might think 'Why am I thinking this? It must mean that I am a bad/crazy/weird person. Or maybe it means that something bad is going to happen.' In fact, it is really important to know that these thoughts do not mean anything at all – they are just random thoughts that everyone gets.

- We have lots and lots of thoughts every day – some people guess we might have as many as 50,000!

- Thoughts are our mind's way of reacting to things that are happening to us, both outside and inside.

- Sometimes we *choose* to think about things. These are called '*intentional' thoughts* and they are thoughts that we want to have and that we can *control*.

- But sometimes we all experience *intrusive thoughts*. These are thoughts that just 'pop' into our minds. We don't choose to have them and we don't have any control over them – they just happen!

Intrusive thoughts fit into three main categories:

Positive intrusive thoughts:
These are thoughts that are pleasant to have. Can you think of any examples from the last week?

Neutral intrusive thoughts:
These are thoughts that are not pleasant or unpleasant. They are just 'ordinary'. Can you think of any examples from the last week?

 Negative intrusive thoughts:
These are thoughts that are sad, unpleasant or scary to have. Can you think of any examples from the last week?

So, who gets negative intrusive thoughts?

Absolutely EVERYONE!

100% of people get sad, scary, horrible thoughts popping into their minds that they don't want to have and they can't control.

One study asked nearly 300 students to say whether they had experienced certain intrusive thoughts, and a very large number said yes. For example:

- 50 per cent of young people had an intrusive thought about seriously hurting or killing their parents

- 60 per cent had an intrusive thought about strangers naked

- 46 per cent had an intrusive thought about jumping off something high

- 55 per cent had a thought about sex with someone 'unacceptable' e.g. a family member, teacher

Why are intrusive thoughts in OCD so horrible?

- Although **everyone** gets intrusive thoughts, they cause more distress for young people with OCD.

- Their brain tells them that these thoughts are really important and bad, and that they have to do something about them.

- Young people with OCD often feel very responsible for their thoughts (even though they have no control over them).

'It's sort of like the spam filter on an email account. It's like my spam filter doesn't filter out any of the scary, sad or horrible thoughts – it holds on to all of them. It's particularly bad, because it filters out all of the nice thoughts!'

- OCD is particularly cruel, because it gives you thoughts about the very worst things that you could imagine happening. It puts these thoughts into your head over and over again.

'I love my parents so much, but OCD kept putting thoughts in my head that I wanted something horrible to happen to them. I'd see pictures in my mind of them being in a car crash. It happened over and over again.'

Thoughts aren't facts!

- Just because a thought pops into your head, does not mean it's true. Your brain is just coming up with different options and ideas – that's what brains do!

- Having a thought about something bad **does not mean you are a bad person!**

- Having a thought about something bad happening **does not mean that it is going to happen**. In the same way, having a thought about something good happening doesn't mean that we can make it come true!

- Making you worry about these things is a really common OCD trick!

Let's try:

- thinking really hard about winning the lottery or finding money under your chair. Can you make it happen?

- thinking about something bad happening, such as the roof falling down, or a fire starting? Can you make it happen?

If not, why not?

What can we do to fight back?

- Just as with all OCD fears, it's important that we face up to these thoughts and don't run away from them.

- We know that some things make the thoughts worse.

Don't try and push thoughts away.

- Pushing thoughts away (or avoiding them) just tends to make them come back even more strongly!

- Try really hard **NOT** to think about a pink elephant in the room. What do you notice?

- It's like throwing a tennis ball against a wall – the harder you throw it, the harder it comes back!

But some things can be more helpful.

Allow yourself to think about the thought head on

- The best way to fight OCD is to not avoid the horrible thoughts.

- If we allow ourselves to think about them (without doing compulsions), they eventually lose their power. Imagine if you watched the same horror film 50 times, what would happen eventually?

- To fight OCD, we even think about the thoughts on purpose, so that we can get used to them. Eventually, they will stop making us feel anxious.

- Sometimes we can even make a recording of the different thoughts and play them over and over again.

■ **Why not ask some of the people you know (who do not have OCD) about the sorts of upsetting thoughts they sometimes get? Write down what you found out below.**

What did you find out about other people's thoughts (who do not have OCD)?

Tools for fighting OCD

TOOL 10: LEARNING TO LET THOUGHTS GO

Once you've practised the techniques above (e.g. exposing yourself to the thoughts deliberately and not pushing them away), you'll find that **negative intrusive thoughts eventually stop being scary and distressing**.

However, they may still pop into your head at times during the day. If these thoughts no longer cause you anxiety and distress, you can start to respond to them in a new way.

Young people *without* OCD do not tend to pay very much attention when negative thoughts pop into their head:

> 'Sometimes I notice a horrible thought, but I just tend to ignore it and get on with what I'm doing. I might think "eww" or "that's a bit weird" – but I wouldn't really worry about it.'

Thoughts as clouds

- Letting thoughts go can seem really difficult to begin with. One technique that can help is to think of your mind as a *clear blue sky*.

- Sometimes, you'll find that thoughts start to come into your mind – just like clouds passing across the sky.

- Practise just noticing the thoughts as they come in. Just observe them – and say 'oh yes, there's another OCD thought'. It will slowly pass across the sky and disappear.

- Sometimes your sky might be full of clouds. They might be pleasant, pretty, fluffy clouds, or they may be big, black, horrible clouds. But even dark clouds will just pass overhead in the end. Eventually, the sky will be clear and blue again.

- You can't hold on to clouds, you can't grab at them or push them away. All you can do is watch and wait for them to pass.

- **Try practising this with your own thoughts. Can you just notice them, and wait for them to pass overhead?**

Tools for fighting OCD

TOOL 11: RESPONSIBILITY PIE CHARTS

Sometimes OCD tricks us by making us think it is our fault if something awful happens

■ For example, OCD might tell us that if we don't wash our hands four times after touching something with germs on it, then Mum or Dad will get sick.

■ OCD tells us that we will be 100 per cent responsible for them becoming sick because of not washing our hands four times.

■ We can use our own knowledge and experience to boss OCD back when it makes us feel responsible for something awful happening.

■ If OCD tells us that it is 100 per cent our fault if Mum or Dad gets sick, all we need to do is think of what possible reasons there are for Mum or Dad getting sick.

 Then we would need to list all possible reasons below, putting your role at the bottom of the list.

> Example:
>
> 1. Illness caught from someone at work.
>
> 2. Caught out in the wind or rain without a coat.
>
> 3. Stress and being run down.
>
> 4. Not washing my hands four times after touching things with germs on.

Now, draw a 'pie chart' and divide up your pie, giving each of the possible reasons a slice of pie that represents a rough percentage of responsibility for the outcome occurring.

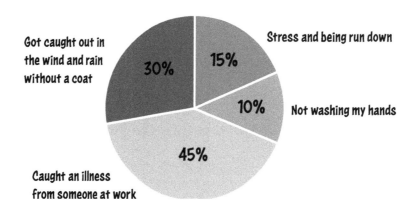

Sometimes OCD tricks us by making us think it is our fault if something awful happens

■ What awful things does OCD tell you that you will be responsible for?

_____

_____

_____

■ How much does OCD tell you that you would be responsible for this happening?

_____

_____

_____

■ What are the possible reasons that might account for this happening? Remember to put yourself at the end of the list.

_____

_____

_____

■ Now draw a pie chart, giving each possible reason a slice of pie.

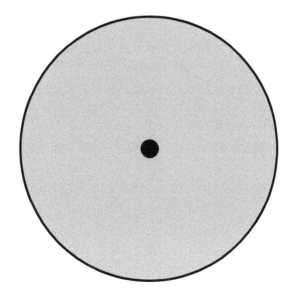

■ What did you learn from this? What did you learn about OCD? How can we test this out further?

Sometimes OCD tricks us by making us think it is our fault if something awful happens

■ What awful things does OCD tell you that you will be responsible for?

_____

_____

_____

■ How much does OCD tell you that you would be responsible for this happening?

_____

_____

_____

■ What are the possible reasons that might account for this happening? Remember to put yourself at the end of the list.

_____

_____

_____

■ Now draw a pie chart, giving each possible reason a slice of pie.

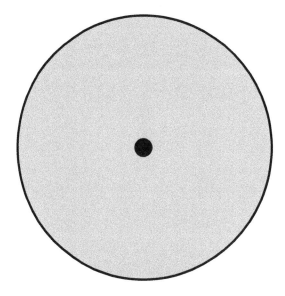

■ What did you learn from this? What did you learn about OCD? How can we test this out further?

Tools for fighting OCD

Tool 12: Don't believe in OCD – find out for yourself

OCD is a liar!

- It tells us all sorts of things that are not true and sometimes it convinces us that our OCD thoughts and behaviour are acceptable and really everyone else should be acting and thinking this way too!

- When you are anxious and having lots of intrusive thoughts or are in the middle of doing compulsions, you may find it very hard not to believe OCD.

- If OCD is lying to you then it may be helpful to find out the truth and to remind yourself of what is 'normal' rather than keep on listening to OCD lies.

Finding out the facts: do your research

- Due to OCD, you may believe something that is simply not true and OCD has convinced you to be far more anxious about something than you need to be.

- For example, OCD might be telling you that you need to avoid urine at all costs because if you come into contact with it you are almost certain to get ill and die.

- Let's look at the facts!

  - Urine is 90 per cent water.

  - Urine is sterile.

  - In Ancient Rome, people would rinse their mouths with urine to whiten their teeth!

- Whatever OCD is saying to you, it may be helpful to go and find out the facts. There are lots of ways to do this. You could talk to your parents or friends. You could do some research on the internet (but make sure you are looking at reliable websites!) or in the library. Or you could ask somebody with expert knowledge, like a doctor or scientist.

- NB – When you find out useful facts like this, *be careful not to keep repeatedly telling yourself them as a way of reassuring yourself* or asking others to keep reassuring you with the facts. Otherwise, sneaky OCD might turn this into a new ritual (e.g. saying to yourself, 'urine is sterile' over and over in your head).

Finding out what's normal: surveys

- OCD sometimes makes us think and behave in unusual ways and after a while you can lose track of what is a 'normal' way to behave and think.

- So, another way to challenge what OCD is saying and telling you to do is to find out what other people think and what other people are doing – this will help to remind you what is a more 'normal' way to behave or think.

- For example, OCD might be telling you that you need to be very thorough when you wash your hands after going to the toilet, using lots of soap and scrubbing them hard for a long time until OCD says they are clean. You might have forgotten how you used to wash your hands before OCD came into your life and have therefore lost sight of what a 'normal' hand wash is like. In this kind of situation, where you are unsure of what is normal, it can be helpful to carry out a survey with your family and friends.

Think of questions to find out what's normal

Examples of the kind of questions you might ask, if you wanted to know about handwashing:

- Do you always wash your hands after going to the toilet?

- When you wash your hands, how long does it take?

- How much soap do you use?

- How do you know when to stop washing your hands?

Here are some top tips for carrying out a survey:

- Think about the questions you want to ask carefully, with the help of your therapist.

- To get a true sense of an average person's experience and what is normal, it is important to carry out the survey with at least five to ten people.

- Write the questions down on paper or set up an online survey so that people can respond anonymously – they might find it hard to be 100 per cent open and honest if you ask them face to face.

- Think about who it would be most helpful to ask to complete the survey. For example, does the age of the person matter, or whether they are male or female?

- If you think you will find it hard to ask your family and friends to complete the survey, your therapist might be able to help by asking people whom they know.

REVIEW
PROGRESS
AND PLAN

HOW'S IT GOING?

■ What has gone well since we last met? Can you list some of the times when you have successfully said 'no' to OCD?

_____

_____

_____

■ What has not gone so well?

_____

_____

_____

■ Have there been any specific difficult times that you'd like us to think about?

_____

_____

_____

■ What symptoms do you still have left?

_____

_____

_____

■ Let's make a plan for how to work on these remaining symptoms.

- Do we need to make a step plan?
- What sort of exposure and response prevention tasks would be helpful?
- What tools do you need to help you?
- Do you need other people to help? What can their role be?
- When are you going to do these tasks?
- How often are you going to do them?
- Would it be helpful to do another overlearning task?

MY ACTION PLAN

- Who can I ask to help me? What can their role be? What could they say to me that would be helpful?

- What tools can I use to fight OCD?

- When am I going to practise fighting?

- How often am I going to do these tasks?

- What could my overlearning task be?

LOOK TO THE FUTURE

- Remember that OCD might try to sneak back into your life at a time of stress or change.

> Things coming up in my life are:

- What is your action plan going to be if OCD does try to sneak back in?

_____

_____

_____

_____

_____

- Remember always to act early.

- What are you looking forward to doing in the next few months without OCD bothering you so much?

- How can you make sure that you achieve these other 'life goals'?

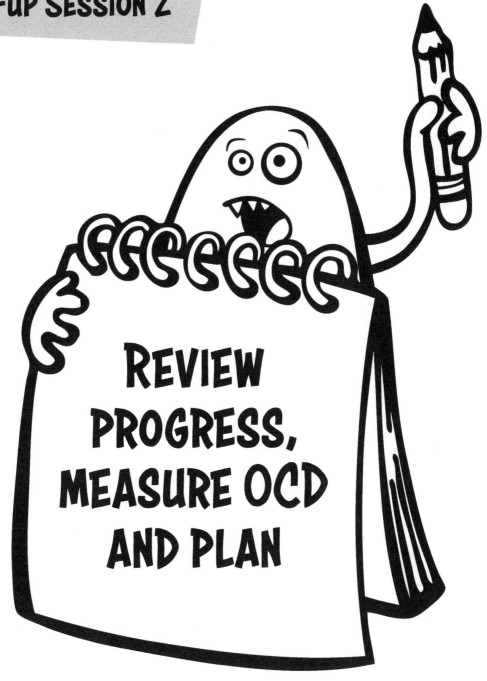

REVIEW
PROGRESS,
MEASURE OCD
AND PLAN

HOW'S IT GOING?

■ What has gone well since we last met? Can you list some of the times when you have successfully said 'no' to OCD?

_____

_____

_____

_____

■ What has not gone so well?

_____

_____

_____

■ Have there been any specific difficult times that you'd like us to think about?

_____

_____

_____

■ What symptoms do you still have left? At this review session, it may be helpful to re-measure your OCD. Your therapist may use some time to do this in the session, or ask you to complete measures before you come.

_____

_____

_____

■ Let's make a plan for how to work on these remaining symptoms.
  • Do we need to make a step plan?
  • What sort of exposure and response prevention tasks would be helpful?
  • What tools do you need to help you?
  • Do you need other people to help? What can their role be?
  • When are you going to do these tasks?
  • How often are you going to do them?
  • Would it be helpful to do another overlearning task?

My Action Plan

- Who can I ask to help me? What can their role be? What could they say to me that would be helpful?

- What tools can I use to fight OCD?

- When am I going to practise fighting?

- How often am I going to do these tasks?

- What could my overlearning task be?

LOOK TO THE FUTURE

- Remember that OCD might try to sneak back into your life at a time of stress or change.

Things coming up in my life are:

- What is your action plan going to be if OCD does try to sneak back in?

_____

_____

_____

_____

_____

- Remember always to act early.

- What are you looking forward to doing in the next few months without OCD bothering you so much?

- How can you make sure that you achieve these other 'life goals'?

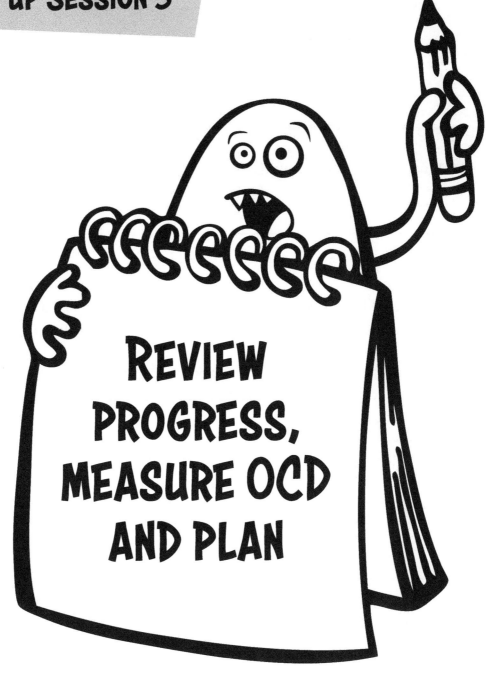

REVIEW
PROGRESS,
MEASURE OCD
AND PLAN

HOW'S IT GOING?

■ What has gone well since we last met? Can you list some of the times when you have successfully said 'no' to OCD?

_____

_____

_____

_____

■ What has not gone so well?

_____

_____

_____

■ Have there been any specific difficult times that you'd like us to think about?

_____

_____

_____

■ What symptoms do you still have left? At this review session, it may be helpful to re-measure your OCD. Your therapist may use some time to do this in the session, or ask you to complete measures before you come.

_____

_____

_____

■ Let's make a plan for how to work on these remaining symptoms.
  • Do we need to make a step plan?
  • What sort of exposure and response prevention tasks would be helpful?
  • What tools do you need to help you?
  • Do you need other people to help? What can their role be?
  • When are you going to do these tasks?
  • How often are you going to do them?
  • Would it be helpful to do another overlearning task?

MY ACTION PLAN

- ■ Who can I ask to help me? What can their role be? What could they say to me that would be helpful?

- ■ What tools can I use to fight OCD?

- ■ When am I going to practise fighting?

- ■ How often am I going to do these tasks?

- ■ What could my overlearning task be?

LOOK TO THE FUTURE

■ Remember that OCD might try to sneak back into your life at a time of stress or change.

> 🖊 Things coming up in my life are:

■ What is your action plan going to be if OCD does try to sneak back in?

_____

_____

_____

_____

_____

■ Remember always to act early.

■ What are you looking forward to doing in the next few months without OCD bothering you so much?

■ How can you make sure that you achieve these other 'life goals'?

REVIEW PROGRESS, MEASURE OCD AND PLAN

HOW'S IT GOING?

■ What has gone well since we last met? Can you list some of the times when you have successfully said 'no' to OCD?

_____

_____

_____

_____

■ What has not gone so well?

_____

_____

_____

■ Have there been any specific difficult times that you'd like us to think about?

_____

_____

_____

■ What symptoms do you still have left? At this review session, it may be helpful to re-measure your OCD. Your therapist may use some time to do this in the session, or ask you to complete measures before you come.

_____

_____

_____

■ Let's make a plan for how to work on these remaining symptoms.
  • Do we need to make a step plan?
  • What sort of exposure and response prevention tasks would be helpful?
  • What tools do you need to help you?
  • Do you need other people to help? What can their role be?
  • When are you going to do these tasks?
  • How often are you going to do them?
  • Would it be helpful to do another overlearning task?

MY ACTION PLAN

- Who can I ask to help me? What can their role be? What could they say to me that would be helpful?

- What tools can I use to fight OCD?

- When am I going to practise fighting?

- How often am I going to do these tasks?

- What could my overlearning task be?

LOOK TO THE FUTURE

■ Remember that OCD might try to sneak back into your life at a time of stress or change.

> 🖉 Things coming up in my life are:

■ What is your action plan going to be if OCD does try to sneak back in?

_____

_____

_____

_____

_____

■ Remember always to act early.

■ What are you looking forward to doing in the next few months without OCD bothering you so much?

■ How can you make sure that you achieve these other 'life goals'?

OCD – Tools to Help Young People Fight Back!
A CBT Manual for Therapists

Cynthia Turner, Georgina Krebs and Chloë Volz
Illustrated by Lisa Jo Robinson

Paperback: £25.00 / $40.00
ISBN: 978 1 84905 403 4
eISBN: 978 0 85700 771 1
48 pages

Obsessive compulsive disorder (OCD) affects approximately one in a hundred young people, and often makes it difficult to lead happy and productive lives. This manual from the distinguished Maudsley hospital guides therapists through the process of treating young people with the disorder and supporting patients and their families.

Designed to be used in conjunction with the complementary workbook *OCD – Tools to Help You Fight Back!*, it features an adaptable evidence-based treatment based on cognitive behavioural therapy and exposure and response prevention techniques. It provides instructions on how best to educate young people and their families about OCD and anxiety, and on how to involve patients' families in the recovery process to form a truly collaborative team.

Essential reading for professionals treating young people with OCD, it will prove a valuable resource for both experienced therapists and clinicians in training.

Dr Cynthia Turner is a Psychologist who holds Honorary Lecturer positions at the University of Queensland and the Institute of Psychiatry at Kings College London, and is an Honorary Consultant Clinical Psychologist at the Maudsley.

Chloë Volz is a Consultant Clinical Psychologist and Team Lead at the National and Specialist OCD, BDD and Related Disorders Service at the Maudsley Hospital, UK where she has worked since 2002.

Georgina Krebs holds a Clinical Research Training Fellowship at the Institute of Psychiatry, Psychology and Neuroscience and is an Honorary Principal Clinical Psychologist at the OCD, BDD and Related Disorders Service at the Maudsley Hospital.